Building Confidence and Improving Behavior in Children

A Guide for Parents and Teachers

RACHEL WISE

CONTENTS

1. TOP FIVE REASONS FOR BEHAVIOR PROBLEMS IN KIDS

This chapter is helpful for any adult (teacher, parent, caregiver, etc.) who has a child with behavioral difficulties. Remember, there are no magic answers, and some kids may have challenging behavior no matter what strategies you use. However, most kids respond well to positive behavior strategies and these should be your first step in trying to help your child. Note: If you feel your child's behavior is out of control and you have done everything you can, it is recommended that you seek the help of a medical and/or mental health professional.

An important thing to remember is that generally behaviors (positive or negative) serve a purpose. The purpose or reason for the behavior is called the *function*. Professionals often conduct functional behavior assessments to determine the function of problematic behavior and put strategies in place to prevent or alleviate the problem.

Here is a basic example of determining the function of a behavior and implementing strategies to help: a child who frequently has a runny nose might keep using their sleeve to wipe it. If this child never learned to use a tissue or doesn't have access to tissues, the behavior will continue because the child is not comfortable when their face is not clean. Giving them access to tissues and teaching them to use tissues could alleviate the problem. If you punished the child, rather than providing them with the appropriate tools, you will likely be unsuccessful at stopping the behavior because you haven't addressed the need/function. If the punishment does work (the child stops out of fear), the child will likely be very uncomfortable. This can lead to more problematic behaviors because they still won't have the tools to address the problem.

Because children are often punished for their behavior without getting the tools to address their needs, punishment often leads to more behavior problems. The premise of positive behavior support is that children are taught replacement skills and are provided with a supportive environment to minimize problematic behaviors, rather than being punished in an attempt to force them to stop doing something.

People often say that kids who aren't punished for their negative behavior act out, but that is because many adults don't know how else to handle the behavior. Many kids who are punished act better in the short term out of fear, but the behaviors often return, happen when parents/teachers aren't around, or evolve into a different kind of problem.

As a parent, teacher, caregiver, etc., you can do your own functional behavior assessment (trying to figure out the reason for the behavior) and put strategies in place to support your child and give them the tools they need to be successful. To do a functional behavior assessment, analyze the behavior in different environments. Questions you need to ask include: "What is the specific behavior you are concerned about?" "When does it happen?" (e.g., does it happen when a demand is given, when other kids are around, when they can't have what they want, when they don't have a structured activity, when they are with a specific person, etc.) "How is the behavior handled by the adults?" "What is the child getting out of the behavior?" Once you have a hypothesis as to the reason for the behavior, you can target the child's specific needs.

Here are five common reasons that children act out, along with specific strategies to address the child's needs and help alleviate the behavior.

Reason 1: The child is trying to get more control over their environment. Many kids feel they have little control. They are often being told what to do by others and many times are expected to follow directions without question even if they don't agree with them.

Imagine that your day was planned by someone else and you were frequently told, "No, you can't do that," "You can't have that," "You must stop that," or "You must do this now!" Feeling in control of one's own life is an essential key to happiness. Some kids do whatever they can to feel in control—even if it means lying to get what they want, breaking rules, refusing to follow your directions, throwing a tantrum to get out of something or to obtain something, or arguing with you.

What to do about it: Give your child as much control over their environment as possible. As long as they are not hurting themsleves or anyone else, disrespecting others, damaging property, or being inconsiderate of other people or their belongings, allow them to pursue their interests, play how they want to, get creative, and make a mess. Also, include choices in their day, ask their opinion about things, and let them know what will happen next. When your child can't have something, explain the reason why, empathize with their feelings, and offer an alternative. Set up expectations ahead of time (a chart may be helpful—i.e., complete homework, set table, take out garbage) and allow your child to earn privileges for good/compliant behavior rather than threaten to take privileges away. This puts the ball in their court, giving them the power to work for the things they enjoy, thus giving them more control over their environment. If possible, allow them to *alternate* preferred with non-preferred activities (for example, homework, TV, set table, eat dinner, computer time, take out garbage, iPad, bed). When your child feels they have control, they will spend less time trying to exhibit control. Don't give attention to tantrums, but ensure your child's and others' safety during the tantrum. Be flexible with choices, encourage strengths, but also make sure to stick to your rules. If you have a rule and are set on it (e.g., first homework, then TV) don't spend time negotiating or arguing with your child. This teaches them that they can get you to bend the rules if they keep asking and pressing.

Reason 2: The child is trying to feel good about him/herself and validate their worthiness. Kids who feel inferior, have low self-esteem, and need to gain acceptance may do inappropriate things to get your or others' attention. An example may be the student always cracking jokes in class, the kid who moons their brother and sister, the one who keeps saying something inappropriate no matter how many times you ask them to stop. These kids may also do other things to make themselves feel worthy, like picking on their little brother, doing something dangerous just to feel cool, or negatively judging others.

What to do about it: Remove attention from the negative behaviors and focus on the positive ones. If your child is getting the attention of their siblings or classmates for behavior, do the best you can to encourage them to not pay attention to the inappropriate/negative behavior. Instead, work to build up the child's self-esteem and give attention for good, appropriate, positive behavior. Try to provide your child with positive social role models. Set rules regarding behavioral expectations and give your child positive feedback for following those rules (phrase rules in the positive by telling your child what to do instead of what not to do). Focus on your child's strengths and give them plenty of opportunities to pursue their interests. Do not tolerate any bullying or teasing in your household/classroom. Remind children who are bullying/teasing that they must treat everyone with respect and direct them to another room if they continue being mean to others. Stress that you are a family/team and everyone needs to be supportive of each other.

Reason 3: The child has a need to move, burn energy, or stimulate himself in some way. An example is a child who constantly is running and jumping on furniture in the house no matter how many times you say "relax," "stop," or "sit down."

What to do about it: Give your child plenty of outlets to burn energy. Can they jump rope, jump on a trampoline, be your running partner, do a dance video? Give your child regularly scheduled outlets for exercise. Again, post house rules (e.g., walk nicely in the house), and give positive attention for following those rules. Provide your child with meaningful activities (utilizing their strengths) so they are not looking for something to do. Children with time on their hands are much more likely to run and jump in the house than children focused on an activity they enjoy such as doing an art project, helping mom cook in the kitchen, or learning how to use the computer. This is also true for children in school. A child engrossed in a hands-on activity is much more likely to be focused and calm than a child who is forced to sit in their seat and listen to an hour lecture.

Reason 4: You are giving the child more than they can handle. An example is a four-year-old who refuses to clean up their room, a seven-year-old who refuses to do their homework, or a five-year-old who keeps running away or grabbing toys in the supermarket line. Many young children and some older children (such as those with ADHD) have trouble organizing belongings, focusing on homework for long stretches of time, or waiting quietly.

What to do about it: Try to get to know what your child is capable of before putting demands on them. Additionally, you may need to provide assistance to help your child through the task. For example, have your child clean up one toy before taking out another so they don't get overwhelmed with cleaning up a lot at once, or give specific instructions (e.g., put the block in bin, put your shirts in that drawer—some kids benefit from a written list with breaks after completing a few things on the list), give your child breaks during lengthy homework tasks (e.g., complete the first ten problems, take a five-minute break and complete the next ten, or bring your child something to occupy themself in the supermarket line).

Reason 5: The child is frustrated/angry about something and cannot express him/herself. Some children act in aggressive ways (to themselves and/or others when they can't tell/explain how they feel or what they need). This may happen with young children or children with speech/language impairments or other special needs, such as autism or an intellectual disability. Some children may have difficulty expressing themselves due to anxiety or fear of being judged, yelled at, punished, or ignored.

What to do about it: For children who cannot express themselves due to speech/language impairments or simply being young in age, utilize pictures, gestures, etc., to help them tell you how they feel or what they want. Offer them choices by showing them the objects you are offering and offer alternatives rather than just saying "no" to their requests and behaviors. Teach them an alternative to express frustration, such as squeezing a stress ball, biting a safe object (for children who bite when frustrated), or pointing to a picture of how they feel. For children who do not have speech/language needs but do not express themselves due to anxiety, fear, or inexperience, help build their self-esteem by showing them that their thoughts, feelings and frustrations are valid and they matter. Focus on their strengths, and try to empathize with what they may be going through. Try the best you can to put yourself in their shoes and work with them rather than punish them for doing something you deem wrong.

Do not tolerate aggressive behavior. Remind the child to keep his/her hands to him/herself and that hitting is unacceptable. Try to identify with what they might be going through or encourage them to express how they feel. If the child continues to be aggressive, keep everyone safe by maintaining distance. Create a barrier if needed, such as standing on the other side of a table, or holding up a pillow to block kicks or hits. If you are able, move them to a safe space to cool down where they can't hurt anyone. Allow them to join others only when they regains control.

If you have concerns about the safety of yourself, your child, or anyone else, call 911 or the crisis number in your area.

Keep in Mind:
- While this chapter gives some very effective strategies for alleviating behavior problems, I am sure you can find functions of behavior, problematic situations, or behavior strategies that are not covered here. Whatever the situation, try to determine the function of the behavior and provide strategies to support your child's needs. Every child is different, so try to tailor your behavioral supports to your child's unique strengths, interests, and personality.

- Sometimes several functions of behavior may all be happening at the same time. For example, you may have a child who refuses to follow directions and complete tasks, makes fun of other people, has a lot of energy, and has trouble expressing how they feel. To tackle all of these behaviors at once you would employ a combination of the strategies above.
- What one person deems bad/wrong another might not. Try to think about whether you could simply let something go or provide support, rather than reacting negatively/judging the child, etc. Think of the reasons you have done things that other people got mad at you for. Do you think you should be punished for them?
- Work with all children to develop positive ways to express/cope with their frustration or anger (e.g., saying how they feel, walking away, exercising, doing something they enjoy).

2. HOW TO TALK TO KIDS TO IMPROVE BEHAVIOR

Twenty years of experience has taught me that being calm, encouraging, positive, patient, and consistent far outweighs yelling, punishing, and threatening in any situation with any child, regardless of what you believe has or hasn't worked in the past. Research and experience show that positive parenting/teaching strategies win every time. And why is that?

Just like adults, kids want their opinions, feelings, ideas, and choices to be heard, validated, and at least sometimes honored. Many times adults push kids' feelings to the side: "I don't care how you feel." "You will do it because I said so." Some children handle this type of treatment well and still grow up to be kindhearted, responsible adults. Other children, especially those who are very strong-willed will push back and fight you to the death, regardless of how much you yell, punish, or medicate them. And my question is, Can you blame them?

Yes, they are children and are expected to respect "authority," but just like adults, if something does not feel right to them, they resist it. It is the nature of freewill that is "human nature."

Compromising, meeting a child halfway, and being understanding about just how little control they have and what frustration this causes, is key. Through this type of thinking, you can provide a child with as much freedom and independence as possible while still guiding them to make good choices, have good values, and eventually be productive, contributing members of society.

When anyone feels like their feelings are ignored or dismissed, thoughts are not heard, and desires are not cared about, they feel frustrated, angry, and disappointed. A lifetime of frustration, anger, and sadness leads to one miserable adult. And when you are miserable, you feel like nothing matters. When you are depressed, anxious and angry at the world, you are not at your best. And how can we make good choices when we are jaded by a lifetime of dismissed feelings?

How do I know all of this? I know because it happened to me. My mission is to uplift people's spirits with the hope of creating an overall positive change in the world. We should all be working towards the common goal of a peaceful planet. Starting at the very core, our children, is the key to making this happen.

While there are many ways to promote positive behavior in kids, this chapter focuses on the way you say certain things to children. First, I will give some negative examples that I have heard over and over again over the years, followed by some positive examples that often lead to cooperative, pleasant and positive behavior. Think about which kind of talking you most often do with your kids and how it may affect their behavior.

Examples of Negative Statements

- If you don't clean your room, I am throwing all your toys in the garbage!
- I don't care what you want. Turn off your game and go to bed now!
- That's it! You didn't share! Get in the corner now and don't come out until I say so!
- You're interrupting me while I am talking to an adult! Are you kidding me? How dare you? Sit down now and don't get up till I say so.
- Put your head down and don't move!
- Stop being a baby! I don't care if you don't like the food. You'll eat what I give you!
- Oh God, you're such a crybaby.

While some may think that people don't really talk

this way, it is extremely common and actually appears to be a more popular parenting style than using positive language. I have also frequently observed this type of language in the classroom. No person, child or adult wants to be spoken to like this.

Examples of Positive Statements

Specific Praise
- You worked so hard on cleaning your room today.
- I love how you are trying new foods. You ate really well at lunch.
- That was so nice of you to share your blocks with your sister.
- Wow! That was a great choice when you helped clean up the game pieces!
- You worked so hard on your math homework! You should be so proud of yourself!

Empathetic Statements/Choice:
- I know you are upset because your sister will not share her snack with you. It is frustrating when you can't get what you want. Can I get you a snack? Would you like grapes or yogurt?
- I know you don't like doing your homework. Is there anything I can help you with? Let's break it into small parts and

you can take breaks to do something fun. Here, do ten math problems and then you can color or watch a video for five minutes before completing the next ten.

- I understand that you are mad because you don't want to put your toys away and go to bed. Choose one toy to hold while we get in bed and read a story. You can pick the story too.
- Good sleep is important and tomorrow there will be time to play again.

People often say, "Kids need to learn the way the real world works" or "People aren't going to be helpful or understanding and kids need to learn how to deal with it." Is that the kind of world we want? Do we want to settle for an unpleasant world and say that we need to be harsh with our kids in order to prepare them, or do we want to do something about it? The number one thing that will make the world a better place is to make it all about the kids and constantly treat them with the respect that we constantly demand from them. If they grow up with confidence and happiness, they will most likely grow up to make healthy choices, leading to an overall improvement in society.

You may disagree this advice, but nothing will change what I have witnessed myself, with a 99-percent success rate, for more than 19 years. Yes, there will always be children who have challenging behavior issues even with all the right strategies in place. But if you haven't used positive behavior support as a first step, don't assume that a child has behavior problems or needs psychiatric treatment.

3. SEVENTEEN WAYS TO GET YOUR KIDS TO LISTEN TO YOU AND SHOW YOU RESPECT

This chapter gives you tips that help you get your kids to listen to you, show you respect and connect with you. Working as a residential counselor, behavior specialist, school psychologist, assistant teacher, tutor, mobile therapist, and babysitter, I have used all the strategies in this chapter with my own clients and students (except the ones that are more appropriate for the parent-child relationship), and these are the strategies that have been the most effective for getting children to listen to my rules and directions, show me respect, and connect with me. I also know parents and teachers who use many of these strategies and have had great success. With my own young son, I use the strategies that apply for his age level, and I can't wait to continue to use them all as he grows.

In my profession I have often heard comments such as "This won't work because of . . .," "There is no time for this," or "We are coddling our kids too much; it's not like this in the real world." This is what I say to comments like those: There is no magic answer. All we can do is try our best. I know that for me, yelling, punishment and lectures don't work for getting kids to listen, show respect, or connect, whereas these strategies do. As far as things not being like this in the real world, they should be. Here it goes . . .

1. Set expectations for your child and allow them to earn privileges, rather than taking privileges away after they do not follow your expectations. For example, tell your child that after school every day they can eat a snack and then they have to do their homework. After homework they can do an activity of their choice (e.g., watch TV, play with toys, go on the computer, etc.). This is much more effective than pressuring a child to do their homework, and then saying "That's it. You're not watching TV!" when they don't complete it. Children are much more cooperative when they know the expectations ahead of time and have the power to earn something than when they are being threatened that something will be taken away.

2. Be consistent and always follow through (barring unforeseen circumstances). If you tell your child

that they can earn a privilege for completing certain tasks or meeting certain expectations, stick to what you said (e.g., first homework, then TV), and make sure you give the earned privilege after the task is completed. If you do not allow your child to earn the privileges you promised, they will not take you or your rules seriously. You also need to stay strong. When they push you ("I don't want to do my homework!") and try to turn on the television, give a reminder in a confident, neutral tone: "Homework first, then TV."

3. Keep calm. While it is human nature to get upset, do your best to keep a calm tone when enforcing your rules with your child. You can stick to what you say without yelling. Enforcing rules without yelling teaches your child that it is possible to stay calm and still get things accomplished, even when you are frustrated or things aren't going your way. This is a great example to set for your child.

4. Encourage and allow creativity even if you think it is too messy. If your child wants to play in the dirt or make a milk-ketchup concoction, let them. Messes can always be cleaned up. If your child is old enough to clean up their own messes, make sure they know ahead of time that they will be expected to clean up when they are done. Make sure they clean up before moving on to an activity of their choice. Keep in mind that some children, especially younger children,

may need help cleaning up.

5. Give your child choices. Children often seek control over their environment because they are frequently told what to do. Give your child choices you are comfortable with (e.g., "Do you want to wear the green shirt or red shirt?" "Do you want jelly or butter on your bagel?" "Do you want to do your math or reading homework first?").

6. Tell your child what to do, instead of what not to do. Research shows that children (even teenagers) respond better to specific directions than to being told not to do something.

Some examples include:

- "Keep working on your homework" rather than "Stop daydreaming."
- "Here, draw on this paper" rather than "Stop drawing on the walls."
- "Hand me my purse" rather than "Stop going in my purse."
- "Walk nicely in the house" rather than "Stop running in the house."

Don't say "Can you ..." when giving a direction, such as "Can you walk nicely in the house?" Give the direction as a statement (Walk nicely ...) and say it with confidence.

7. Take an interest when your child tells you something about their thoughts, feelings, ideas or just

about their day. Children are often excited to tell their parents something (e.g., "Guess what my teacher said in class today?" "I think I know what I want to be when I grow up." "If I were President, I would make sure there were no more bad guys."). No matter how insignificant you think it is or if you simply don't feel like listening, show an interest anyway. When your kids know you listen and care about what they say, they will come to you about important stuff, the stuff you want them to tell you about. It also helps their self-esteem and confidence to feel like what they say matters. Kids with good self-esteem and self-confidence make better choices in general.

8. Take an interest when your child shows you something they did. Working as a school psychologist over the years, and even among my own friends, I have seen many kids show their parents a picture they drew or a dance move they learned, only for the parent to not say anything. Children want to feel like we care about the things they are excited about, the things they did for the first time, the things they did by themselves, or the things they created. Even if you think it is no big deal, it is a big deal to them and that should be enough to make it a big deal for you. Again, this helps with confidence and self-esteem.

9. Acknowledge when your child puts forth good effort. People like to hear when they did something right, and this includes children. When people know

they are doing the right things and pleasing others, they want to do more of it. Some examples for acknowledging effort include: "You worked really hard on cleaning your room; it looks great," "I saw you studying really hard for that test; you really put a lot of effort into it," "I know you don't like sharing your toys with your brother, but I saw you sharing really nicely with him this morning! Keep up the good work!" Even if your child does not seem to care or does not seem pleased by the praise, do it anyway. Their reaction on the outside may not match how they feel on the inside.

10. Let your child know that you understand when they are upset about something (show empathy). Examples include: "I know you are upset that you didn't get invited to that birthday party; it hurts not to feel included" or "I know this homework assignment is frustrating you; let me see how I can help you with it."

11. Listen to your child's side of the story. If you get a phone call from another parent or a teacher about something your child did wrong, take the time to hear what your child has to say. Even if your child was wrong, it is important for them to feel heard by you, and you may get to know your child a little better in the process. You can also use the opportunity as a teaching moment. For example, if your child kept talking in class to a friend because they were upset

about something that happened at recess, talk to your child about alternative strategies they could have used, other than disrupting the class (e.g., asking to talk to a guidance counselor, talking to their friend at the end of the day, talking to you about it after school, etc.). This would also be a good time to remind your child that even when we are upset or don't agree with something, we still have to follow the rules.

12. Tell your child about you. While some things are your personal business and not meant for your child's ears, kids feel connected to their parents when their parents can open up to them. For example, tell them about your school days, your hobbies, your dreams. Your child will be more likely to open up to you if you can open up to them.

13. Make time to do things with your child. We are all busy. Some days fly by so fast that it seems like you've got nothing done on your to-do list, yet you haven't sat down once. In the midst of this craziness we call life, find time. Whether it is five minutes a day or a few hours on the weekend, spend quality time with your child. Some examples of quality time could include talking about your day, watching a movie to-gether, reading a book together, going to the park, going out for dinner, cooking together, fixing some-thing or making something together, etc. If your child does not want to do these things with you, still ask, make an effort, make yourself available, and keep try-

ing.

14. Show your child what good behavior looks like. Children often get punished for behavior rather than being taught or shown an alternative strategy or different behavior. Here is an example: Teach your child how to ask for things. If you see your child snatch a toy from another child, teach them how to ask for the toy rather than yelling at them or punishing them for snatching the toy. Show them how to ask and have them practice it. Next time you see your child asking nicely for a toy, acknowledge the behavior (e.g., "That was really nice when you asked Michael if you could play with his toy").

15. Encourage your child to be independent. Let your child do as much as they can on their own, providing assistance only when necessary. One strategy I love, is to wait for the child to ask for help before offering it. I have watched a child struggle to get the wrapper off his juice box straw on several occasions. Rather than saying "Here, let me help you," I would simply wait to see what they would do. Sometimes they would ask for help, other times they would eventually get it on their own. In some instances the child would get frustrated, throw down the straw and say, "I can't do it." This led to a perfect opportunity to teach the child how to ask for help.

16. Notice possible hidden talents. Sometimes children do things that we find annoying that could

actually be channeled into something positive. For example, a kid who always wants to run in the house might be a good candidate to be your running partner. A child who is always banging on the table might do well at the drums. Ask your child if they would like to try something positive, rather than getting frustrated and annoyed at the behavior.

17. Say "Good morning," and "Goodnight" (or some variation of those) and "I love you" every day. We all get busy, but this is an important one. Feeling loved, wanted, noticed, and acknowledged by our parents is one of the best things for our self-esteem. Even if you are not the lovey-dovey type, do it for your child. Make time for affection too (hugs, kisses, etc.). Older children may not want affection, but making an effort to give a hug or even asking for hug is a great way to show you care.

Keep in mind that for some children, they may actually get more resistant when you try new strategies. You may need to be consistent over a period of time before you see change. Also, even if you don't get the results you hoped for, know that you are doing your part to use positive strategies to help your child. If things feel out of control, seek help from a mental health or medical professional.

4. ARE YOU USING THIS NUMBER ONE STRATEGY TO GET YOUR CHILDREN TO LISTEN?

In my training as a school psychologist, I learned about a concept called *positive phrasing, also* referred to as *positive language.* In my career as both a school psychologist and behavior specialist, I have noticed that people sometimes confuse positive phrasing with praise or positive reinforcement. While they are both considered positive ways to support behavior, positive phrasing refers specifically to phrasing directives in a positive way (by giving a clear specific directive rather than just telling a child *stop, no,* or *don't),* whereas praise, also an effective strategy, is specific positive feedback for making good choices (e.g., "I am impressed by how hard you worked on your math assignment").

Research studies support the use of both positive phrasing and specific praise. For instance, the Responsive Classroom approach, which focuses heavily on the use of positive phrasing and praise, is an evidenced-based approach that has been shown to significantly improve students' academics and behavior in the classroom. Working in the fields of academics and behavior for the past 20 years, and now having been a mother for the past six years, I consistently have experienced the benefits of positive phrasing.

In general, children respond much better to positive phrasing for a few reasons:

- It sounds more supportive and makes the child less likely to challenge you or push back.
- It provides the child with an alternative that they may struggle to think of on their own. Just saying *stop* or *don't* doesn't provide insight into what the child can do instead. Some children need to be provided with that alternative.
- Directions are clear and concise so there is no confusion about what the child is expected to do.

Below are 11 commonly used negative phrases (in bold type). Beneath each are clear examples of positive alternatives that you can say or do.

"Stop running"
- "Walk nicely"
- "Walking feet"
- "Walk in the halls"
- "You can run when we go to the park, when you are in the gym," etc.

"Stop jumping"
- Offer a place where the child can jump
- Provide an alternative (jumping jacks, jump rope)
- "Keep your feet on the ground"

"Stop playing with that/sit still"
- Some people actually focus better when fidgeting, so consider letting it go
- If the behavior is disruptive, teach the child a way that they can move (e.g., squeeze and relax fingers, wiggle toes, feel belly breathe) or offer something they can play with that would not be disruptive (e.g., bouncy bands on chair, fidget jewelry, pencil topper)

"Stop screaming"
- "Use an inside voice"
- "Go in your room and shut the door if you need to get your screaming out"

"Don't hit/push/kick"
- "Hands to yourself"
- "Use your words"
- "Take some space"

"Don't touch that"
- "Leave that there"
- "Put that down"
- "Show me where that goes"
- "Here, have this instead"

"Stop teasing your sister/brother"
- "Speak respectfully"
- "Speak kindly"
- "Say something nice"

"Don't play with your food"
- "Eat your food"
- "Let's put your food away; you must be done"
- "I see you are done; pick a toy to play with"

"Stop talking"
- "Listen to the speaker"
- "Focus on your work"
- "Finish writing your sentence"

"Stop fighting"

- "You both seem angry; take a break/space for yourself and let's talk about how we can solve this when you feel a little better"
- "What do you need?"
- "How can we resolve this?"
- "Write down in words or draw a picture of what you think is causing your anger/frustration, then we can talk about it"

"No, you can't do that/No, you can't have that"

- "You can have that after lunch"
- "You can do that when we get back from Grandma's house"
- "I am not able to buy that, but you can play with this"
- "You can have this instead"
- "You can do this instead"

Some people are skeptical about this approach, but once you start using it, it will become second nature and you will personally see the benefits of positive phrasing. You can practice it when the kids aren't around to get the hang of it. Also, an explanation can go a long way, such as "The reason you can't touch that is because _____, but you can do this . . ." Adults often say, "I don't need to give a reason. You should do it because I said so." But it is human nature to want to understand the reason for things. It is a learning experience for children to be taught why it is important to follow certain rules and expectations, and just like adults, kids are curious about the world around them and why things work the way they do. When kids understand the reason for things, they are more likely to comply with a request.

When you simply keep telling a child to stop doing something, and you become louder and louder because they are not listening, it turns into a battle and someone will eventually give in. This is a power struggle approach, and for the child, it does not lead to a clear understanding or to the importance of the request. Once the threat of yelling or punishment is removed, the negative behavior often returns. Positive phrasing allows you to teach your child behavioral expectations in a supportive way, in order to help them internalize the importance of these behavioral expectations.

Since not all people use the approach of positive phrasing, I talk to my four-year-old about different ways adults might communicate the same message. I realize that not all the authority figures in his life will use this approach. We talk about what he can do when he hears other adults saying *stop, no* and *don't,* but in our house, positive phrasing is the approach we use and it is very effective. As he is now older, I sometimes pair a negative with a positive so he has a better understanding of negative phrasing. But when he was very young I always stuck with only the positive. An example of pairing negative and positive is "Stop screaming because your sister is sleeping; use your inside voice."

Sometimes I demonstrate concepts like inside voice, walking nicely, using words to express frustration, etc., so he is even more familiar and comfortable with the concepts. Positive phrasing and demonstration are the same approaches I have used, very successfully, with my students and clients over the past 20 years. Sometimes picture cards—that show children behaving well (walking nicely, keeping their hands to themselves, etc.)—are helpful too.

While positive phrasing is helpful for getting kids to listen, it is not a magical fix for every child. It is important to remember that usually various strategies need to be combined in order to see changes in behavior.

5. TEN SIMPLE WAYS TO IMPROVE CHILDREN'S BEHAVIOR (AT HOME OR AT SCHOOL)

Parents and teachers often wonder how to discipline a child with behavior problems. Although some children truly have challenging behaviors regardless of what strategies we try, many children simply need to have the adults in their lives make changes in the way they react, respond or interact with them. This chapter gives ten simple strategies that you can start implementing right now to encourage positive behavior in your child or students. All of these strategies are positive in nature and will help you connect with your child or students in a way that will increase their confidence, self-respect and respect for you. Children with good confidence and a healthy respect for themselves and for the adults in their lives show better cooperation and make healthier choices.

Below are ten simple strategies to promote positive behavior.

1. Verbally acknowledge children's efforts. Tell your child/student specifically what they did that you are proud of. For example, you can say, "You were so focused on your math homework tonight! Keep up the good work," "That was so nice the way you helped your brother with his math homework." When children get praised for doing the right thing, they want to do more of it. Virtually all children want to please adults (whether they show it or not), so for most children, praise makes a positive impact. Praise is also an easy way to give your child the attention many children so desperately crave.

2. Use positive body language to show approval for positive behavior. Positive body language can include a smile, thumbs-up, high-five, pat on the back, etc. Keep in mind that some children do not like to be touched and would respond better to something like a thumbs-up than a pat on the back. Get to know your child/student to know what they like.

3. Use humor with your child/student. Make jokes, listen to their jokes, smile often, say something silly, sing something you would normally speak, or do anything else that might make them smile or laugh (make

sure it is age appropriate).

4. Show your child/student that you are happy to see them. Smile at them when they come into the room. For parents, put your arms out to invite a hug. Ask about their day, weekend, etc., and really listen when they talk.

5. Remind your child/student that they should be proud of themselves (e.g., "You worked so hard on that science project. You should be so proud of yourself!"). This helps build confidence in them, so they can learn to be proud of themselves for being persistent, working hard, being kind to others, etc. If they feel successful, they will be successful.

6. Take an interest in your child's/student's interests. Ask them what they enjoy, get excited about their creations or accomplishments, ask them what they want to learn about, ask them their opinion about things, etc. Teachers, try to incorporate students' interests in the classroom. Parents, do activities with your children (academic or otherwise) that involve something they are interested in, even if it may not be your favorite activity. Let them choose topics of interest for certain activities.

7. Acknowledge your child's/student's feelings with empathy. Be understanding when they are nervous because they are trying something for the first

time, frustrated because a writing assignment is difficult for them, disappointed because they didn't get invited to a birthday party, or embarrassed because other students laughed at them. Avoid saying things like "Stop making a big deal about it," "You'll get over it," or "Why are you having such a hard time with this; it's easy." Instead, make empathetic statements like "I understand that this assignment is frustrating for you" or "I understand that you are nervous; that's common when trying something new." Also, let them know that you are there to help in any way you can.

8. Be open-minded and don't pass judgment on your child/student if their thoughts, values, feelings or ideas don't match yours. Of course, it is okay to share your opinion (that unsafe or hurtful behavior is unacceptable), but in general, don't make them wrong for their opinion. They need to feel that they can be open and be themselves around the adults in their lives. When children feel like they won't be judged or made wrong, they are more likely to talk to adults when there is a real problem.

9. Be a role model for good behavior. If you want your child to treat others with respect, you do the same. If you want your child to be an honest person, set an example of honesty for them.

10. Follow through on your promises and rules

(barring unforeseen consequences), and stay away from empty threats. If you tell your child/student that they can pick a favorite book to read after they finish their math assignment, make sure you stick to your end of the bargain. If you tell your child that they can go on the computer after their sister has a turn, make sure they get a chance to do that.

Have consistent rules that teach your child that they need to stick to their end of the bargain as well. For example, if you have a rule such as "Homework first, then TV," stick to that rule by making sure your child completes their homework before watching TV.

If your child is significantly struggling with behavior, despite positive strategies being in place, talk to your child's doctor or a mental health professional to help determine the next steps you should take. If you are a teacher who is having significant behavioral difficulties with a student (despite several positive strategies), talk to the child's parent and your school team (administrator, guidance counselor, etc.).

Always keep in mind that some children truly have difficulty controlling their behaviors or making better choices because they have not yet learned more acceptable methods to get their point across, or because their behavior happens so quickly (almost impulsively) that they haven't had the opportunity to slow down and think of an alternative. This often happens when children feel anxious, scared, sad or angry. While this is frustrating for adults, imagine how it feels to the child who frequently gets punished, singled out, or yelled at because they don't have the coping skills, communication skills or control to do something different.

Stay away from empty threats such as "If you don't stop, I am going to leave you here" or "I'll throw all of your toys away if you don't clean them up." These statements can be scary for children and can cause crying, tantrums, etc., and in all probability you are not going to do those things. If you keep making empty threats, your child will learn that you don't mean what you say and will also learn to not take you seriously. If your child/student has faith in what you say and knows the boundaries you have set for them, they will feel a sense of security and trust, which leads to confidence in themselves and respect for you. Children with confidence and respect feel good about themselves and the people around them, and confident, respectful children are more likely to cooperate with requests and make healthy choices.

6. HOW TO USE NATURAL AND LOGICAL CONSEQUENCES TO IMPROVE CHILDREN'S BEHAVIOR

Natural consequences are consequences that occur naturally as the result of a behavior. For instance, if you were talking and being loud in a movie theater, people might yell at you or tell you to be quiet (so that other people can hear the movie). If you are hitting your friends, they probably won't want to play with you (because it hurts). It is helpful for kids to know expectations ahead of time, but in many cases we learn as we go.

Some natural consequences work all on their own. For instance, when I was five I touched an iron and burned my finger. That was a natural consequence and I never did it again.

Logical consequences are those imposed by teachers,

parents or other authority figures, and they fit the behavior in a logical way (hence the name). For instance, if a student draws on the desk, a logical consequence would be to tell them that they need to clean it before joining the fun art project (or even before going home). If your child hits you when angry, a logical consequence would be to tell them to keep their hands to themself and move away from them, or block yourself until they are calm (even if that means removing them to a safe area where they can't hurt anyone).

Once they are calm and can talk rationally, empathize with what made them angry, but also let them know how it made you feel to be hit and that hitting is not tolerated under any circumstances because it hurts. Then discuss alternatives for what they should do next time they are angry, rather than hitting (this can be done through discussion, drawings, pictures, etc). You may even wish to have them role play the scenario over and practice the new strategy.

This consequence should be a requirement before your child moves on to an activity of their choice. Be consistent and implement consequences the same way each time. If hitting is a major problem, you could even step it up a notch and say, "You need to keep your hands to yourself for x amount of time if you want to earn the time to do _____ (insert activity that your child enjoys) today. Privileges do not come free. There are certain expectations that we all need to follow to get to do the things we enjoy.

It is very easy and effective to state logical consequences in the positive, such as, "We need to clean the desk first and then you can join the art activity" (after the student draws all over the desk). Or, "First we need to work together to come up with alternative strategies, and then you can move on to your desired activity, because hitting is never allowed." If the child is not ready, wait it out. They want to do the things they enjoy, but they must take the imposed consequence first (first you must do this/then you can do that).

Since natural and logical consequences make sense, they lead to less resistance and reduce the power struggle. You can set the expectations ahead of time and implement the consequences when needed (e.g., "If you break something, you need to fix it or earn the money to get it fixed or replaced"; "If you steal something, you need to return it in person to its original owner").

It is easy to stay calm when implementing these consequences because you know you are doing the right thing. You do not need to yell or scream, but you also should not budge from your position. Also, when your child is calm and in a good mood, it is a great time to talk about replacement behaviors and the purpose of rules (e.g., what should we do if we want to talk in a theater, what should we do it we feel angry, what are acceptable things to draw on, what are the things we are allowed to use our hands for, what is the purpose of these rules, why do we have rules, etc.). When you see your child implementing those replacement behaviors, give them positive feedback! "You sat so quietly through the movie! Keep up the good work!"

I consistently see the effectiveness of explaining natural and logical consequences in the positive, so that they become something that the child is working towards rather than something that is being taken away. No one responds well to threats, especially when they don't feel they are in the wrong (which is often the case when people are told they did something wrong). When you try to use power and threats to change behavior, you often get resistance because the child wants to feel in control, which is natural. When they can earn things and when they feel they are learning practical skills, they are more likely to feel in control.

No one is perfect and you may not be able to think of the natural or logical consequence in every single scenario, but try your best to do so. These consequences are practical and apply to real life. For instance, if you go to work, follow directions and work hard, you will earn your paycheck. If you pay your bills you can keep your car, your house, etc. If you keep your hands to yourself and only take other people's belongings when you have permission, you will stay out of jail. Keep in mind phrases like "first this, then that" rather than "if you don't do this you can't do that." What scenarios can you think of in which you can use natural and logical consequences to shape and guide behavior?

Using natural and logical consequences is not something that everyone *must* do. You can continue to use regular punishment (like timeouts or taking away privileges) or reward systems (like sticker charts), but if you continue to feel frustrated and don't see a change, it is best to try to implement these strategies as much as possible. As a behavior specialist, school psychologist, and mother, I personally endorse them as being the most effective, based on my own experiences and research. They may take time to take effect. Be consistent, stick to your guns, and don't expect change overnight.

7. PRACTICAL STRATEGIES TO DECREASE IMPULSIVE BEHAVIORS IN CHILDREN

Impulsive behaviors can make everyday situations challenging for children and the people in their lives. Impulsive behaviors are defined as actions that occur quickly and seem to happen without thought or consideration of the consequences. Children diagnosed with ADHD (attention deficit hyperactivity disorder) often engage in impulsive behaviors, but impulsive behaviors do not necessarily indicate that a person has ADHD.

These are some examples of impulsive behaviors:

- Hitting someone or throwing objects when angry

- Jumping off a dangerously high surface
- Throwing papers in class
- Running in the library
- Grabbing materials off a shelf in a store
- Interrupting/disrupting others while they are talking or working
- Stealing

Below are nine strategies to decrease impulsive behaviors.

1. Outline behavioral expectations for upcoming situations. What should behavior look and sound like? What will the activity consist of? For instance, if you are going to a restaurant, talk about what will happen when you get there (e.g., wait to be seated, look at the menu, order your food, etc.) and about what your child's behavior should look like (e.g., using an inside voice, speaking respectfully while inside the restaurant, waiting nicely for your food). Let your child know you are pleased when you observe them following the behavioral expectations appropriately (e.g., "You are waiting very nicely for the food").

2. Work with your child to develop self-awareness about their behavior and problem-solving skills. When you and your child have a free moment to talk and are both in a relaxed mood, help your child get to know their impulsive behaviors, how they affects themself and others, and what alternative behaviors

they could consider.

Things to think/talk about when exploring self-awareness with your child as it relates to impulsive behavior:

- When do they tend to act impulsively?
- How does it affect them?
- How does it affect others?
- What can they do to ensure they don't make impulsive decisions during their trouble spots?
- How can emotions affect impulsivity?
- What are some alternative ways to handle their emotions?

Research suggests that children with impulsive behaviors—such as those diagnosed with ADHD or ODD (oppositional defiant disorder)—show improvement when consistently taught pro-social behaviors, such as how to conduct themselves in various situations, how to identify problems and brainstorm solutions, and how to recognize which behaviors may be undesirable in certain situations.

3. Have your child reward themself with a preferred activity or item if they've gotten through a specific time period (e.g., dinner, school or homework) without any impulsive behaviors (behaviors that disrupt the environment or are hurtful/inconsiderate to self or others).

4. Encourage your child to observe their environment to notice if they see or hear impulsive behaviors. Talk about what the individual could have done differently. Discuss the situation and alternatives.

5. Talk about the differences between impulsive and non-impulsive behaviors/decisions. Try to visualize through real-life examples what those differences look like. Act out, show pictures, or draw different scenarios. A Google search will provide numerous images that illustrate impulsive and non-impulsive behaviors. For a fun activity, ask your child to draw a picture of someone engaging in an impulsive and a non-impulsive behavior.

6. Children who have more down-time/unstructured time are more likely to engage in impulsive behaviors. Help your child plan their day so they knows what to do with themself. Fill the day with preferred activities (playing outside, video games, coloring, music) and non-preferred activities (homework, chores, etc.). Remember: Less down time equals fewer impulsive behaviors.

7. Explain to your child that once they get to be an adult, impulsive behaviors are often not tolerated in the workplace or community. Discuss real-life consequences, such as being fired, thrown out or arrested for certain types of impulsive behaviors (e.g.,

throwing things in a public place, hitting someone at work, etc.).

8. Encourage your child to exercise. Studies show that regular exercise helps reduce anxiety and hyper-activity, both of which can put a child at risk for impulsive behaviors.

9. Accept that you will not be able to make all im-pulsive behaviors go away. Some individuals simply have a somewhat impulsive personality, and while you want to make behaviors more appropriate, you don't want to stop a person from being who they are. Everybody can be a little impulsive at times, and in certain situations it can be a good thing. But keep in mind that if the impulsive behavior is inconsider-ate, hurtful, or disrespectful to self or others, it should be addressed.

8. TOP TEN DISCIPLINE TIPS FOR KIDS WITH OPPOSITIONAL DEFIANT DISORDER

Raising a child with *oppositional defiant disorder* (ODD) can be extremely frustrating because you feel like everything is a constant battle. You want your child to do their homework, pick up their toys, get dressed for school, etc., and you are constantly faced with refusal.

As a behavior specialist and school psychologist I have had many parents and teachers ask for advice on how to handle this kind of defiant behavior. In my training I learned a lot about positive behavior support strategies and have used them with my clients and students for the past 18 years, and now with my own son. I can tell you firsthand that these strategies are extremely effective. They work when I use them and when I teach others how to use them with their children or students. People often think that positive behavior support is simply giving rewards for good behavior, and when that doesn't work they think that the system doesn't work. I have repeatedly heard that positive behavior support does not work from people who were not using it correctly. While a piece of positive behavior support is allowing children to earn privileges rather than taking them away, it is so much more than just that. It is a way of speaking, acting, and responding to behavior.

My top ten tips are summarized below. These tips, incidentally, are effective for all kids, not just those diagnosed with ODD.

1. Set up expectations ahead of time and allow your child to earn privileges for following those expectations. This is much more effective for encouraging compliance than punishing your child or taking away privileges when they don't do what you want them to do.

Let your child have a say in what they want to work for. Allowing children to earn privileges puts the ball in their court. They know what is expected and they know what they have to do to earn the things they enjoy. They also feel a sense of pride when they earn what they worked for.

When your child starts getting off track, remind them of what they are working toward rather than telling them what you will take away if they don't listen. Research shows that children and adolescents are much more likely do what is expected when they have the power to earn something than when they are being threatened that you will take something from them.

2. Use transition warnings to let your child know what is coming next. Here is an example: "In ten minutes it is time to turn off your video games and come eat dinner" or "After this show it is time for homework." Give some more reminders as the time is winding down (e.g., "In two minutes it's time for dinner"). A timer or visual timer can be helpful for children who don't have a concept of time.

3. Use empathetic statements to show your child you understand how they feel. Imagine how you would feel if someone came into your room and said, "Get off the computer and go to bed." Although they are kids and are expected to follow adults' rules, they still have the same feelings you would have in that type of situation. You can show them you understand how they feel with a statement such as "I know you are really enjoying your computer time and you don't want to turn it off, but you need to get rest for school tomorrow. You can have some time on the computer again tomorrow."

4. Phrase directives in the positive and remove the word *can*. For example, instead of saying "Stop jump-

ing on the furniture" or "Can you stop jumping on the furniture?" try something like "Sit down" or "Come down off the couch" in a calm but confident tone. If possible provide an alternative activity or redirect them to something they like to do, like "Let's do jumping jacks together" or "Here are some puzzles to play with." Children respond much better when you tell them *what* to do rather than what *not* to do. Anything you want your child to stop, you can phrase in the positive by giving them a clear direction of what you want them to do. Giving an explanation such as "You can fall" or "That can damage the couch" is often helpful as well.

5. Use specific praise when your child follows your expectations or listens to your directions. Some examples include "Excellent job picking up your toys," "You were so focused during homework tonight," "Nice job listening to directions," etc. Specific praise or acknowledgement of healthy behaviors reminds the child what behaviors you are looking for and reinforces them.

6. Pick your battles. If your five-year-old is playing in the dirt and you find it disgusting, allow it. As long as they are safe, not hurting or disrespecting themself or anyone else, and not damaging anything, try to give them as much freedom as possible.

7. Give your child choices whenever possible. Examples include "Do you want to wear the green or

amples include "Do you want to wear the green or red shirt?" "Do you want to do your math or reading homework first?" "Do you want to set the table or take out the garbage?"

8. Say what you mean and mean what you say. If you tell your child that they need to pick up they toys before they can play outside, make sure you follow through on your rule and honor your end of the bargain. Stay away from empty threats (punishments that you will never follow through on). Your child will come to learn the value of your words. If you don't mean what you say, they won't take you seriously.

9. If possible, utilize a schedule with your child that builds in chores, homework (if applicable), self-help tasks (shower, brush teeth, etc.), and fun activities. Have your child participate in creating the schedule. Embed the fun activities into the schedule so that your child alternates between preferred and non-preferred activities. One part of the schedule needs to be complete before moving on to the next part. Also, keep in mind that children with idle time on their hands are looking for things to do, so structuring their time can alleviate some impulsive behaviors like running/jumping in the house.

10. Avoid arguing, long lectures or sarcastic remarks about your child's behavior. Stick to your rules and don't negotiate, go back and forth, or argue with

your child. If your child starts to argue or throws a tantrum after you have stated the rule and shown empathy, let them know that you are not going to discuss it anymore. Do not give attention to a temper tantrum. Once the tantrum is over you can praise your child for calming down, provide empathy again if needed, and listen if your child wants to talk about their feelings. Then direct your child back to the task they are expected to do.

If your child is acting in an unsafe manner, protect them and others from harm, but do not try to negotiate with your child or give in to a tantrum in order to make it stop. This will only lead to more tantrums in the future. If you are ever concerned for the safety of your child or anyone else's, contact the crisis center or emergency number in your area.

Additional Information:

Research suggests that children with ADHD and ODD who display impulsive behaviors (e.g., acting without thinking, hitting, yelling, blurting something out, taking something without asking, breaking something, etc.), show improvement when positive behavior support strategies such as the ones discussed above are used in conjunction with strategies that teach pro-social behaviors (e.g., how to conduct oneself in various situations, how to identify problems and brainstorm solutions, how to recognize which behaviors may be undesirable in certain situations and why). While there is no one method that works for every child, personal experience has proven just how effective the above methods are.

9. HOW TO CONTOL TEMPER TANTRUMS AT HOME AND SCHOOL (PART 1)

This chapter illustrates ways for adults to change their own behaviors in order to prevent and appropriately respond to temper tantrums. In my experience, parents or teachers who work with children with behavior challenges are often surprised to hear that they have to change their own behaviors or change the environment to meet the needs of the child. As a behavior consultant, I have often heard, "Why should I have to change? He is the one acting out." Or, "It is too much work to make these changes." In actuality, if the adult does not make any changes in their own behavior or the environment, it is very unlikely that the child's behavior will change.

Keep in mind that behavioral strategies do not always lead to immediate change in a child's behavior. Your child or student may be surprised by the new strategies you are using, and behaviors could become even more challenging at first. You need to employ strategies consistently over a period of time to see their true effect on behavior.

Temper tantrums are a normal part of a developing child's life. They generally occur in young children (four and under), but also may occur in older children, especially children with difficulty expressing their feelings or communicating their thoughts, wants, and needs.

Tantrums happen when children feel a lack of control in their world. As adults, we have found our own ways to vent our frustrations when things don't go our way. Many children have not yet developed these skills. Because they have trouble identifying, understanding or appropriately expressing their frustrations, they have tantrums as a way to vent their feelings.

Temper tantrums can be frustrating for both you and your child. They sometimes last for a long time (anywhere from a couple of minutes to an hour or more). They can be very loud and scary. You may also feel bad that your child is so unhappy, and you just want it to stop.

Below are some common reasons children have tantrums

- They want something they can't have (e.g., "No, you can't play with Brian today," "No, you can't have any more candy").
- They are scared to go someplace or do something new, or they are anxious about your leaving them (e.g., "I am taking you to the doctor," "You are going to a new school," "I am going out and you will stay with Aunt Sue").
- They are told they have to do something they don't want to do (e.g., "You have to go to bed now," "You need to complete your math homework").
- They are yelled at for misbehaving or told they have to stop their behavior (e.g., "Stop throwing the ball in the house," "Don't touch my purse").
- They are told to stop doing something they enjoy, or told to do something they don't enjoy (e.g., "Stop playing with your toys and go to bed").

Here are four common adult responses, and outcomes, to child temper tantrums:

1. Reasoning with the child to get them to see that the tantrum is unnecessary and that it needs to stop. Once a child begins a tantrum, they are almost impossible to reason with. Trying to talk them out of it usually leads to more crying, screaming, etc.

2. Giving in to the child, just to make the tantrum stop. Although this works in the short term, it teaches the child that they can use tantrums to get their way. This will lead to more tantrums in the future.

3. Trying to negotiate with the child. Here is an example: You and your child already agreed that you are going to the store for food and they can pick out one toy. When you get to the store, they see three toys they want and start begging for all three. You negotiate and say, "How about if I buy you two instead?" If you made an agreement, or you have a rule set in place, change the rule or agreement only if you determine that your rule was unreasonable. Negotiating and changing rules or agreements reinforces to your child that they can get you to bend the rules by having a tantrum, and teaches them that you don't necessarily mean what you say. This can lead to their not taking your rules seriously.

4. Resorting to yelling or spanking. This type of reaction could cause the tantrum to get worse. If it does stop the tantrum in the short term, it could lead to more feelings of anger or anxiety in the child, ultimately leading to more tantrums or other types of challenging behaviors in the long term, such as shutting down or not communicating thoughts or feelings.

Remember to take precautions. If tantrums seem

constant, unsafe, or feel unmanageable to you, tell your child's doctor. They should be able to provide you with additional resources to help you and your child or refer you to someone who can. If this is happening with a child in your class, request additional support from your school team (guidance counselor, administrator, etc.) and tell the child's parents what is happening.

Now let's look at situations mentioned above and talk about how to prevent a tantrum for each type of scenario.

Scenario 1: Your child wants something they can't have. Rather than just saying no, use the EECR approach (Empathetic Statement, Explanation, Choice, Reminder). Let's look at an example: Your child asks for more candy after you already told them they can have only one piece a day because you want them to eat food that is good for them (and candy is not). They already had their piece of candy for the day, but they come to you asking for more.

<u>Empathetic Statement</u>: "I understand you want more candy because it tastes so good" (making them feel understood).

<u>Explanation</u>: "For healthy minds and bodies, it is important to eat food that is good for us" (reiterating the rule or explaining the reason).

<u>Choice</u>: "If you're hungry, you can have an apple or yogurt" (making them feel valuable, giving them a sense of control).

<u>Reminder</u>: "You can have a piece of candy again

tomorrow" (reminding them that they will enjoy some candy again soon). This step would not apply if your child is trying to get to something that they can never have (e.g., something unsafe). If that is the case, still use empathy, explanation, and choice.

It is important to tell the child what is expected (e.g., "For healthy minds and bodies, it is important to eat food that is good for us") rather than what is not expected (e.g., "You can't have candy because it is bad for you"). This type of negative phrasing leaves more room for arguing or talking back.

Language may need to be shortened or modified for young children or children who have language-based difficulties. (e.g., instead of saying no, show empathy and offer a choice). Very young children or children who have language-based difficulties may have trouble visualizing the choices, and they may benefit from being shown their choices.

People often have a hard time giving up the word *no* because they feel children need to accept it without argument since this will be expected in the "real world" when they grow up. This is an unrealistic expectation on the part of the adult. Children often have a hard time seeing past the word *no* and thinking of alternatives to meet their needs. This is why they beg and plead. Without seeing the whole picture, they get stuck on the fact that they can't have something.

People often say that parents who don't say *no* end up with spoiled kids. This can be true if you give your kids whatever they want. But using a "what is expected" rather than a "what is not expected" approach allows the parent or teacher to remain in control while helping the child feel respected and understood. It also helps the child visualize other scenarios than the one they are hoping for, which leads to an ability to better accept *no* as they get older.

This approach may sound like a lot of work compared to just saying the one word *no,* but it saves a lot of time because children who get this type of response are much less likely to argue, beg, cry or have a tantrum.

Scenario 2: Your child is scared to go someplace or do something new, or they are anxious about your leaving them. Prepare your child for the upcoming situation. Tell them what to expect, so they are not surprised. Obviously you can't predict everything, but try your best. For children with language difficulties, pictures can help them understand what to expect. Social stories (e.g., stories that explain what an event will be like, such as a doctor's visit or the first day of school) are a great tool to prepare a child for these types of situations. Social stories can also be used to teach children about behavioral expectations, such as how to act in a store, restaurant or movie theater. Social stories can be found online. You can also create your own social stories by using drawings or photos, and/or by writing down relevant information. Consider your child's developmental level when designing or obtaining social stories.

Sometimes pictures and words in a story are not

enough to prepare a child. Some children need one or more practice visits before the actual event.

Let the child know exactly when the event will happen and give them reminders as it is getting closer (e.g., "We are going to the doctor today. Do you have any questions about what it will be like?" or "I am going out tonight and you will stay with Aunt Sue. Do you have questions?").

Empathize with your child's feelings (e.g., "I understand going to the doctor can be scary for you") rather than dismissing their feelings (e.g., "You don't have to be afraid; it's not scary").

And once again, simplifying language or using pictures can help with children with language-based difficulties.

Let your child know that they did well after the event is over (e.g., "I know going to the doctor was scary for you, but you did it anyway. Nice work! You should feel proud").

If you have to leave your child for the day or evening, reassure your child that you will be back, be empathetic about their feelings ("I understand you are scared to be without me, but you will be taken care of by Aunt Sue and I will be back after dinner") and hug and kiss your child before you go (if they like that type of affection). You can leave a picture of yourself with your child, or another object that they associate with you, if you find that helps.

When you return, be affectionate and act excited to see your child. If applicable, let them know that you are proud of them and they should be proud of themselves for behaving appropriately or staying calm while you were gone. If your child is having a tantrum as you are trying to get out the door, do not prolong leaving or try to get your child to accept that you are leaving as this will likely prolong the tantrum; just go. Most children will adjust quickly once you have actually left.

Scenario 3: Your child is told to do something that they don't want to do. To prevent a tantrum, prepare your child for upcoming changes and try to stick to a routine when possible so your child knows what to expect. For example, you can read your child a story each night and let them know ahead of time that after the story is bedtime. For an older child, you can let them have a half hour of computer time before bed and let them know that after the computer time will be bedtime. Children are less likely to argue or throw a tantrum when they know what to expect and they have had time to mentally prepare themselves.

Children with language-based difficulties or those with trouble understanding the concept of time do well when activities have a definitive ending (e.g. "When this show is over, it is time for bed" rather than "It is bed time in a half an hour"). If your child is doing something without a definitive ending, such as browsing the Internet, using a timer can be helpful.

Children who get overwhelmed or frustrated, or simply do not want to complete homework, chores or other tasks often benefit from breaks during the work and earned privileges upon completion. For example, if you want your child to complete 20 math problems, try saying, "Do ten problems, take a five-minute break to do an activity of choice, then do the next ten problems. When you are done, you can watch a show." Stay away from language like, "If you don't do your math homework, you are not watching TV." This sets the stage for talking back, not listening to you, and tantrums. Children respond much better when they can earn privileges (e.g., "After your math homework, you can watch TV.").

Scenario 4: Your child is yelled at for misbehaving or told that they must stop their behavior (e.g., "Stop jumping on the couch!").

Rather than yelling or telling your child to stop the behavior, give a directive phrased in the positive, in a neutral, confident tone (e.g., "Come down off the couch") and/or redirect your child to a different activity, providing choice (e.g., "You may jump on your trampoline or use your jump rope."). Children are much more likely to respond to your requests when you tell them what to do instead of what not to do, because the new direction gives them an alternative, which young children often have trouble finding on their own. An explanation can be helpful as well to help them understand your perspective or the reason for the directive (e.g., that jumping might break the furniture). If they argue, stick to your rule and do not go back and forth with them about it. After your child complies with you, acknowledge their compliance (e.g., "Thank you for following directions").

Scenario 5: Your child is told to stop doing something they enjoy or to do something they don't enjoy. Use the same strategies listed in Scenario 3. Prepare your child for upcoming changes and try to stick to a routine when possible so your child knows what to expect. For example, you can let your child know that in five minutes it is time to clean up and go to bed, or after the TV show it is time to do dishes, rather than saying "Stop watching TV and go do the dishes"). As previously stated, children are less likely to argue or throw a tantrum when they know what to expect and they have time to mentally prepare themselves. They also respond better to directives phrased in the positive ("After the TV show it is time to do dishes") rather than the negative ("Stop watching TV and go do the dishes").

10. HOW TO CONTROL TEMPER TANTRUMS AT HOME AND SCHOOL (PART 2)

Continuation from previous chapter…

If your child argues, cries, begs, pleads, throws him/herself on the floor, etc., even after implementing the strategies in Part 1, show empathy, but stand firm in your decision (e.g., "I understand you are scared to go to the doctor, but we are still going because we have to take care of your health"). After you have shown empathy once and enforced your rule or directive, do not engage in discussion about it any further. Sometimes a hug, a joke, or a calming object such as a stuffed animal or stress ball can help your child relax and move on.

However, if your child continues to throw a tantrum after trying these strategies, do not pay attention to the behavior. (Note: for unsafe behaviors that cannot be ignored, there are additional strategies listed below.) You can let your child know that you are not going to argue about it, but then give your child time to move on and calm down on their own). Once your child is calm, it is okay to discuss how the situation made them feel and give them positive feedback for calming down ("I really liked how you calmed yourself down! You should be proud of yourself").

For a child who is extremely upset, or screaming and crying for a prolonged period of time, it is okay to offer them a "tantrum care package." (If they don't want any part of the care package, that is okay.) The package includes tissues to dry their eyes, a drink of water (you would be surprised how taking a drink of water helps many children calm down rather quickly), a hug (if not already offered before, and if it does not exacerbate the situation—sometimes it does) and a calming object if you did not offer it before, or if they did not want it earlier. You can leave these items (water/calming objects) within reach if they decide to use them at some point. Your child might reject these items and scream even louder, but it reminds them that no matter how upset they are, you still care and are there for them. Still continue to wait for them to calm down on their own.

If your child is trying to hurt others or destroy property, move away from them and if possible move any object that they may be able to destroy. Stay in close proximity so you know they are safe, and make sure there are no dangerous objects in the area. Direct away from them, as well, anyone else they are trying to hurt.

If this is not effective and they are still trying to hurt others or destroy property, direct them to a "calm down space," supervise them in the space to ensure safety, but do not give them attention until they have calmed down (i.e., no eye contact, talking, etc.). Again, offering the "tantrum care package" described above is okay.

In extreme situations, some parents like to create a "calm down space" with soft materials like the gym mats. Another fun idea for a calm down space is to fill it with books, stress relieving items (stress balls, fidget toys), a weighted blanket, etc. These are a few examples, but there are a lot of ways to go about creating something like this.

If your child will not go to or stay in the space and continues to engage in unsafe behavior, you may need to hold them so that they can't hurt themself or anyone else or destroy anything. But do not give them attention. Simply hold them until they have calmed down. Let them know that you will let them go once they are safe (e.g., keeping hands and feet to themself, not hurting themself, etc.). This recommendation is only for parents who are comfortable holding their children to keep them safe. You should not be in a position where you are getting hurt. Once your child has calmed down, praise them for regaining control (e.g., "Nice work calming yourself down. I know how upset you were").

In some situations children can be redirected during the tantrum. You can try redirecting your child through humor (e.g., make a joke, sing a silly song, say something in a silly voice), an understanding hug, or by introducing an activity to take their mind off the situation that is causing the frustration (e.g., suggest they play with a favorite toy, do an enjoyable activity, join the family in a game, take deep breaths, count to ten). However, in many cases redirection is not effective and the tantrum continues or even gets worse. If you have tried redirection and it has been unsuccessful, utilize the strategies outlined above—basically, be understanding, give them time to get over it, and do not give in.

If you are out in the community and you cannot ignore the tantrum, take the child out of the store/restaurant to handle the tantrum. If you have a car, you may need to sit with the child in the car until they calm down.

Be consistent with the methods discussed above to let your child know that tantrums do not work. It will take time, patience, and consistency before you see change.

Of course, some children are too large or strong to hold or keep in a safe place. If you have a large child, or any child who is a danger to himself or others, then you need to have an emergency plan. Find out the number to crisis intervention in your area, and in an emergency call crisis intervention or 911. Also, this chapter is not an answer to every situation (it is merely a guide); you may be in a situation where you have tried everything and you don't know where to turn for help. All you can do is try your best and involve family support, community support, and professional support as much as you can.

Handling Tantrums in School:

If you are an educator, you may not be able to ignore a disruptive tantrum because it interferes with other students' learning. Additionally, you may not be comfortable or be allowed to hold a child who is acting unsafe during a tantrum. Therefore, it is important to know your school's policy for handling disruptive, unsafe or destructive behaviors in your classroom or school. Here are some options to suggest to your school if no protocol is in place:

- Have authorized personnel (e.g., principal, vice principal, guidance counselor, security guard, etc.) stay with the child while you remove the other students to a safe location. Remain with your students until you get word that it is safe for you and your students to return.
- Have authorized personnel escort the child to a safe location in the building.
- Authorized personnel should follow the same steps recommended above to keep

the child safe. However, hugging and prolonged holds may not be allowed, and this needs to be discussed with administration.

- For a child who has severe tantrums in school that are unsafe, destructive or excessively disruptive, a clear behavior plan and safety plan should be in place. Behavior plans should include all the positive support strategies listed above and may also include the opportunity to work towards a preferred activity or privilege. Some children are more motivated to control their emotions (not engage in destructive/disruptive behavior) if they know they are working toward something that is fun or meaningful (e.g., computer game, board game with a friend). Also, children are much more likely to comply when they know they are working *toward* something than when they being threatened that you will take something *away*.

- The school counselor may be able to work with the student periodically to discuss effective ways to handle the student's emotions when they are upset, frustrated, etc.

- Your school team should be involved every step of the way to determine what steps to take for a child whose behavior does not improve with all of these supportive strategies.

Tantrums in Very Young Children:

The methods in this chapter are meant for children with more reasoning ability than a child under three, but below I note some strategies to prevent tantrums in children that young.

Strategy 1: Your child wants something they can't have. For example, they want to go into your refrigerator or grab your ceramic cat from the shelf. If possible, try to engage your child in an activity that satisfies their curiosity (e.g., hold them while you point to and name the items in the fridge or take the ceramic cat off the shelf and show it to them with your supervision). If that is not possible, try redirecting them by showing them a toy that interests them, or bring them to a different area and then show them something exciting.

For children that young, out of sight is quickly out of mind. If they are already holding something they can't have, try putting your hand out and act very excited for them to hand it to you or show them where they can put the item, praising them when they do, or offer them a more exciting object. If you have to, for safety reasons, you can also take the object from the child and quickly replace it with a more exciting object or offer them another choice. Again, empathy and understanding can go a long way in these situations.

Strategy 2: Your child is having a tantrum because you are leaving. Reassure your child that you will be back and hug and kiss your child before you go. You can leave a picture of yourself behind or a special object for the babysitter to show your child if you find that helps. When you return, be affectionate and act excited to see your child. Do not prolong leaving or try to get your child to accept that you are leaving, as this will likely prolong the tantrum; just go. Most children will adjust quickly once you have actually left. If it helps you or your child to call and check in, that is a great way to get through the time apart.

Additional Information:

As a general rule, when you observe your children doing the right things, let them know it. This type of positive attention could also lead to a decrease in tantrums. Children thrive on attention. If they don't have enough positive attention, they will use other means to get your attention, even if it is negative.

Use language that helps your child identify their feelings (e.g., "I know your math homework can be frustrating," "Do you feel sad because you can't see your friend today?" "I get that you are mad because your friend yelled at you"). This type of language leads children to be better able to express their feelings. When children can express themselves, they are less likely to throw tantrums.

Children are less likely to have tantrums when they feel a sense of control in their lives. Use choices to help them feel in control (e.g., "Do you want to wear the green shirt or the red one?" "Do you want an apple or banana in your lunch?" "Do you want to do your math or reading homework first?").

When your child is calm and in a pleasant, cooperative mood, talk to them about ways to stay calm when they can't have their way. Give them examples of how to say how they feel (e.g., "I am mad that I can't stay up as late as my brother," "I am scared of the doctor.") Teach them ways to calm down when they are upset (e.g., taking deep breaths, drawing a picture, playing a game, lying on their bed, looking at a book, counting in their head, etc.). For children with repeated unsafe behaviors such as punching and kicking others and destroying property, some therapists suggest teaching alternative behaviors, such as ripping blank paper or punching a pillow. You need to decide what you are comfortable with and assess what alternatives work with your child.

Remember to keep your cool. If you yell, talk in a nasty tone, say mean things or spank your child, it will not lead to a decrease in tantrums, and it could cause other behavior problems. If you want your child's behavior to change, you will have to make changes in your own behavior as a first step.

Finally, I understand that not every one of these strategies will work for you, your household, your classroom, or your child. These strategies may not be what you are used to and may require many changes on your part. While there is no perfect method for eliminating all challenging behaviors, these are the strategies that I endorse and believe in as being the most effective for preventing and handling tantrums.

11. EIGHT MAJOR PRINCIPLES OF POSITIVE BEHAVIOR SUPPORT

While in graduate school for education and school psychology, I learned about the principles of positive behavior support, a research-based practice. At the time, I was working in a group home with individuals with a variety of emotional and behavioral needs. I knew this was the perfect setting to implement my newly learned strategies. I immediately saw the positive impact on my clients, and knew that I would use these strategies to interact with children for the rest of my life, in both professional and personal settings.

As a tutor, mobile therapist, school psychologist, behavior specialist, and mother I have continued to use these strategies with extreme success for many years. Many people think that positive behavior support is nothing more than a reward system, like a sticker chart; and when that doesn't work, they think the process doesn't work. Positive behavior support is so much more. It is a form of communication and it is a science. When you learn to use it in its truest form, you see how effective it truly is.

Major components of positive behavior support include:

1. Telling your child what to do instead of what not to do. For example, instead of saying "Don't run," say "Walk" or "Stay with me" or "Hold my hand." For additional examples, see Chapter 4's bullet list of negative phrases and positive alternatives.

2. Using empathetic statements to show your child that you understand how they feels; for example, if you child requests more candy than the amount allowed, say, "I understand that you want more because it tastes so good, but it's important for your health to eat foods that are good for you."

3. Giving specific positive feedback when you see your child engaging in positive, appropriate behaviors or fulfilling expectations; for example, "Great! You're using your spoon. What nice manners!"

4. Setting expectations ahead of time and allowing your child to work for the things they want rather than punishing/taking things away when they do something you don't approve of (in some cases logi-

cal consequences are necessary, such as removing a child from a situation in which they are hurting someone, or having your child work to earn money to fix something they broke).

5. Giving your child a "heads up" so they know what is coming and know what to expect, rather than making quick/abrupt unexpected changes (this is not always possible, but do your best).

6. Giving your child choices about what to eat, what to wear, what to do first or second, etc. (again, may not be possible every time, but do your best). For young children or children with learning difficulties, providing two to four choices is an appropriate starting point.

7. When expecting your child to perform a task such as cleaning up their room or putting away laundry, working with them and guiding them through the process until they become independent at it (they may need specific instructions about where to put things, and may need large tasks broken down into smaller, manageable steps).

8. Talking to your child about appropriate ways to handle their emotions during a calm/happy period, rather than when they are angry/emotional (the logical and reasoning centers of our brain are not working as productively during angry/emotional states).

These are just some of the principles of positive behavior support, but there are many more.

Positive behavior support and positive parenting are methods that work to teach kids right from wrong using natural and logical consequences (e.g., you make a mess you clean it up; you take something without asking, you give it back; you break something on purpose, you work to earn the money to fix it; you are disruptive in the movie theatre, you leave the theatre).

Positive behavior support methods also acknowledge hard work and effort (you worked so hard on that project, I love the effort you put into your piano lessons, you were such a kind friend to Jessica, etc.). Kids are noticed for the good things they do, and when they are having a hard time, empathy and compassion are used to show kids you are in their corner and understand their point of view, even if you don't agree with their behavior.

Boundaries are set but in a loving and confident way, rather than a scary or threatening way. A true relationship is nurtured. The child feels respected and heard, and in turn the adult is respected and heard. There is a mutual understanding that we are a team (a family, a community, a classroom) and we work together for the good of the group. Certain things do not come free (toys, games, TV, amusement parks), and children understand their role in working toward the things they want to do.

Many people think positive behavior support is a

sticker chart or a reward system. It is not! It is a science that includes a set of rules, and when used correctly, positive behavior support leads to positive effects on behavior. It is a way of talking and behaving, as exemplified below:

- Phrasing things in the positive ("Walk" vs. "Don't run!"
- Acknowledging responsible behavior
- Setting boundaries (if you want to do *x*, you must do *y* first)
- Using natural and logical consequences
- Being empathetic, compassionate and caring
- Working with and relating to your child/student
- Teaching and guiding your child or student by using logical explanations and setting examples, and by demonstrating positive behaviors such as compassion, generosity, helpfulness, thoughtfulness, hard work, empathy, active listening, resiliency, teamwork.

When people feel a sense of belonging, it increases their self-worth, and thus their good choices! Positive and nurturing relationships lead to a sense of belonging at home, in school, and in the community! Positive behavior support is not coddling or treating a child with "kid gloves." It is a scientific way of approaching behavior with the understanding that "bad behavior" is the result of unmet needs along with an unstable set of coping skills and/or communication difficulties. The child needs to be taught coping skills, effective communication, etc., so they can meet their needs in a way that is respectful of others. Punishment does not teach coping skills, communication or any of the other skills sets we want to see our children learn. Positive behavior support is not bribery, stickers for being good, or a lack of discipline. Some children are motivated by stickers and visual charts to represent their progress towards a specific goal; however, bribery and sticker charts are not the foundation of a strong system of positive behavior support.

12. WHAT IS A FUNCTIONAL BEHAVIOR ASSESSMENT AND IS IT EFFECTIVE?

A Functional Behavior Assessment (FBA) is a research-based method used to determine why a child is behaving in a certain way in a school setting; however, an FBA can also be conducted in a residential treatment center or at home if a child is receiving mental health services there. Also, parents can think about ways to use an approach similar to an FBA to address their own child's behavior at home or in the community. Research demonstrates that FBAs are an effective tool for reducing problematic behaviors.

When conducting an FBA a qualified person, such as a behavior specialist or school psychologist, uses several techniques to figure out the cause of behaviors that others (e.g., parents, teacher, administrators) consider inappropriate. Both academic and nonacademic factors are explored in order to develop a hypothesis about what might be causing a child's challenging behavior in the school setting.

Knowing what is behind inappropriate behavior can help the parent or school find ways to modify the environment and to teach the student skills that will help them replace inappropriate behaviors with appropriate ones. The basic idea behind this approach is that the child's behavior serves a purpose. Whether they are aware of it or not, the child acts a certain way to get to a desired outcome or result.

For example, perhaps the child has a hard time showing his work on math problems. In math class, he gets angry, crumples up the paper and throws it on the floor. He's sent to the principal's office.

While the behavior may be considered inappropriate, it served its purpose. The child managed to escape the work that was frustrating him. He may not even realize that that was his goal, but he found a way to deal with the math, which was causing his stress.

A key part of an FBA is figuring out what may trigger certain behaviors. Sometimes parents and teachers think they know what is causing a child's behavior because they've seen other children act in similar ways. However, children can display similar behavior, but for a variety of reasons.

Functional Behavior Assessment vs. Psycho-educational Evaluation:

An FBA has a narrower focus than a psycho-educational evaluation. An FBA examines specific behaviors such as when, where, how and why they happen. A psycho-educational evaluation is a process that's used to determine if a child is eligible for special education services. It looks at all aspects of a child's learning. If behavior is a concern, an FBA may be part of the psycho-educational evaluation process.

The Functional Behavior Assessment Team:

An FBA involves a team of people. A behavior specialist or school psychologist interviews the student's teacher(s), parents, the student himself, the school counselor, and other school staff who may work with the child.

The Steps of a Functional Behavior Assessment:

During an FBA, the team gathers information and uses it to create a behavior plan. The behavior plan will list strategies to modify the environment, teach the child appropriate replacement behaviors, and provide reinforcement for displaying the desired behaviors.

Here are the steps of an FBA:

Step 1: Defining the target behavior
The behavior needs to be defined in clear observ-

able terms. For instance, it is not enough to say a child is aggressive. The person, such as the child's teacher who is describing the behavior needs to be specific (for instance, the child kicks, hits, throws things, etc.).

Step 2: Collecting, comparing and analyzing information

When collecting information, the professional conducting the FBA may review student records, interview teachers, give teachers questionnaires, talk with the student and parents, observe the student, etc.

The professional tries to find answers to such questions as, When and where is the behavior happening, Where is it not happening, How often does the behavior occur, Who is around when it occurs, What seems to happen right before the behavior occurs, What happens after the behavior occurs, What is a more acceptable behavior that can be used as a replacement?

A so-called "ABC chart" is a tool that's frequently used in this step. While observing the student the professional collects data about the (A) Antecedent (what happens before the behavior), the (B) Behavior (the action or reaction), and the (C) Consequence (what happens after the behavior). The consequence does not necessarily refer to a punishment; rather, it looks at what happens after the behavior (e.g., the student is ignored, the student is directed back to their task, friends laugh at the student's behavior, the student is yelled at, etc.).

The student can help provide information about the ABCs too. Only they can share how they truly feel in these situations. Asking a child to try to keep track of what they are feeling—and when—could help the team.

Other tools may include frequency and/or duration charts, which track how often the behaviors occur and how long the behavior lasts. These charts allow you to track the intensity of the behavior as well (generally on a scale of one to ten).

Step 3: Hypothesizing reasons for the behavior
A hypothesis is a guess about why a child is behaving a certain way, based on the data collected. The purpose of the FBA is to determine what the child is escaping, avoiding or getting from the target behavior. As in the example discussed above, the student wanted to avoid the math work that he found too challenging.

Step 4: Developing a plan
Once the team has an understanding of the reason behind the child's behaviors, they create a behavior intervention plan. The plan allows the team to make modifications to the environment, teach replacement behaviors, and provide reinforcement. For instance, in the example discussed above, they may try to make the math problems less frustrating by providing help, peer tutoring, etc. They may work with the child

to get him to ask for help when frustrated. For example, if the child is embarrassed to ask for help, the team may develop a low key way for him to get the help he needs (teacher check ins, student puts an index card on their desk when help is needed, etc.). When the child asks for help and completes the work to the best of their ability, they may be rewarded through positive feedback from the teacher, a break to do a preferred activity, and so on.

Below are examples of how positive strategies are used to improve the child's behavior. All the strategies would be listed in the behavior intervention plan.

Suggestions in a behavior plan can include:

- Changes to the physical environment
- Changes to the way information is taught or presented
- Changes to the child's routine or to events that happen before the inappropriate behavior
- Changes to the consequences for a behavior
- Teaching different, more appropriate behaviors that serve the same purpose (such as asking for help or taking a break when frustrated with math)

The Role of Parents in a Functional Assessment:
Knowing that a child's behavior is causing a prob-

lem at school can bring up many feelings in a parent. However, this process is not about focusing on what your child is doing wrong, but rather about coming up with a solution to help your child with something they are struggling with. Tell the team what behaviors you see at home and what is or is not helpful for your child there. You can keep track of your child's behavior in a journal or by using the ABC approach. Taking notes can make it easier to notice patterns in your child's behavior.

An FBA may not provide an immediate solution to your child's behavior issues, but it can give you a better picture of your child's struggles and of what may help over a period of time. If the strategies are not working, they can be tweaked and the team (which you are a part of) can try something different.

If you think your child needs an FBA, request one through the school principal, who will most likely refer you to the school behavior specialist or school psychologist. If your child attends cyber school—a virtual school, run by a school district or charter school, with assignments posted online and completed work submitted through the school's website—and you have concerns about their behavior as it relates to school, talk to the principal or special education director to find out how an FBA is conducted in the cyber school setting.

13. HOW TO USE SCHEDULES TO IMPROVE CHILDREN'S BEHAVIOR

This chapter discusses how to use schedules with children to promote positive behaviors. Strategies can also be utilized with adults with special needs. Using visual schedules for individuals who may have trouble with reading or language is discussed as well.

Schedules can make a positive difference in a child's behavior in class or at home. When a schedule is in place, children know what is coming next and what is expected of them. Knowing what is coming next lessens anxiety because there is no uncertainty about what they are going to be doing.

As adults, we set up our day and we make our own choices, so we know what is coming next. Imagine doing one thing and having no idea what is going to happen when you are done, or picture someone coming over to you before you are finished with something you enjoy, stopping you from what you are doing, and demanding that you do something else. These situations would stress or frustrate most people. This is often what happens to children when schedules are not in place.

Young children or children with autism or ADHD could get anxious or frustrated when they are directed to do something they were not expecting, or when they abruptly are told to stop a preferred activity.

This could lead to challenging behaviors. They also may have troubling remembering or visualizing if you simply tell them how the day will unfold. A schedule makes it easier to understand, follow and remember the expectations of the day. Also, when a schedule is in place, children get used to their routine.

Although schedules should be slightly varied from day to day to allow for flexibility, they also should be similar enough to allow the child to become comfortable and familiar with their routine. When a child is comfortable in their routine, they also feel less anxious and need fewer reminders from you about what is expected.

When you first initiate the schedule, you may need to give the child several reminders to refer to it (but stay calm so as not to turn the child off to the schedule); but as it becomes a normal part of their day, they may start to check it on their own. The ultimate goal is for the child to become so familiar with the schedule that they start to implement it independently. For

example, let's say your child's schedule upon return-
ing from school is:

- Snack
- Homework for a half an hour
- Ten-minute break for a fun activity
- Homework for another half hour
- Watch TV for a half hour
- Set the table
- Eat dinner
- Play on computer (half hour)
- Tidy up bedroom
- Put on pajamas
- Listen to a story read aloud
- Go to bed

If you consistently implement this schedule, your child can start to implement some of these tasks without your even asking. It will be nice to have your child complete their homework, set the table, and tidy up their room without constant reminders from you. Also, if they are expected to follow the schedule, you are setting up a realistic way to make your child accountable for their own behaviors. If your child is responsible with the schedule, allowing them to have some choice, and/or mixing the order around can be okay, if the tasks are still getting done.

Children often have a lot of expectations to meet. They have trouble being accountable because they have difficulty managing their tasks in an organized way. A schedule allows them to do this. Keep in mind that some children will become overwhelmed with a schedule containing too many steps. In that case, limit the schedule to the few most important things you want the child to accomplish, or cover up steps, revealing only a few steps at a time.

Setting a schedule is also a way of enforcing rules. The rule is that one thing in the schedule must be completed before moving on to the next. If your child tries to use the computer before completing homework, simply refer to the schedule and say, "Remember your schedule; you need to complete your homework first and then you can use the computer."

Blaming the rule on the schedule is a great way to avoid confrontation. It sounds a lot different to a child to hear you refer to a schedule than to hear you say, "You didn't complete your homework so you can't use the computer."

Children who are not used to the approach of enforcing a daily schedule may complain or argue initially, but when they see you are going to implement it consistently and not budge from your position, they will learn to follow the rules. Some children even find it fun to follow and complete the steps in a schedule.

Allow the child to participate in the creation of a home schedule. At school, schedules are often created by the teacher, but they allow the children in the class to participate, if possible. Once the schedule is created, review it thoroughly with the child to the best of their ability to ensure their understanding.

For children with speech and language delays or difficulties, such as those on the autism spectrum, visual schedules with pictures of each activity may work best (ideas for creating picture schedules are found later in this chapter). Children with difficulty understanding language may understand their schedule better if you show them exactly how to use it and practice with them several times. You may need to point to the pictures and actually carry out the tasks with the child before they are able to use it with more independence. Some children may always need reminders to use the schedule, such as pointing to the schedule or walking them over to check the schedule.

To reinforce the schedule, acknowledge the child's efforts when they follow it (e.g., "Great job with your schedule tonight," "Nice work following your schedule," "You were so responsible completing your schedule today," etc.). Children with language difficulties may benefit from a gesture or physical praise (e.g., thumbs up, smile, pat on the back, hug, high five) rather than verbal acknowledgment.

It all depends on the child, though. Some children respond best to verbal praise, some to gestures or physical praise, while others may seem not to respond to praise at all or may not like certain kinds of praise. For children who seem to show no emotion when you praise them, continue to do so anyway because their response on the outside may not match the feeling they get from praise on the inside. Experiment to see what works or doesn't work for your child or student.

For any child following a schedule, you can tie privileges to the completion of the schedule. For example, you can tell the child that they can pick a special activity of their choice once they have completed the schedule or after completing the schedule accurately for a certain number of days.

For children with language difficulties or intellectual disabilities who may not understand that they are working towards earning a privilege, allow them to earn a privilege anyway (something you know they enjoy) after reaching a predetermined goal. For example, if your child loves to watch TV or jump on a trampoline, allow them to earn one of these preferred activities for appropriately utilizing the schedule. Point to the schedule with a smile or thumbs up when they earn the special privilege to help them make the connection.

As an alternative, you can put pictures of preferred activities at the end of the schedule to let a child with language difficulties know that they can choose something they enjoy once they have completed their tasks. Once they earn their preferred activity, allow them to choose the picture of the activity they want to do.

For children who have trouble making choices, you can pick an activity ahead of time that you know the child enjoys, and put a picture of that activity at the end of the schedule. So, if you know your child likes jumping on the trampoline, put a trampoline picture at the end. If they also like television, playing with blocks, etc., alternate the different activities so that they have an opportunity to earn time for the many things they enjoy.

Remember that fun activities can also be built into the schedule itself, such as in the example of the home schedule mentioned previously. Make the expectation you set realistic for the child. For a child with severe behavioral challenges, one day of completing a schedule or even of completing one part of a schedule may be a huge accomplishment and worthy of earning a privilege. For a child with less problematic behaviors, they may be able to go five days with successful schedule completion before earning a very special privilege.

Below are some behaviors to look for that may indicate a schedule will help.

- Significant disorganization in daily activities
- Trouble remembering or figuring out what to do
- Anxiety when routine is disrupted
- Trouble moving on from a preferred activity
- Frequently inattentive or off-task behavior (for off-task students you can point to or remind them of their schedule to redirect them back to task)
- Oppositional or defiant behavior

Place the schedule somewhere the child can always see it. Laminating the schedule, so it does not get ripped or crumpled, can help.

I understand that for parents and teachers with several kids or with many additional responsibilities, a schedule may be hard to keep. Do the best you can, enforcing the rules as best as possible. If it doesn't work for you or your child/student, that is okay. Not every behavioral strategy in this book will work for every child. These strategies are recommendations based what I have seen work and on research.

Below are some options for creating pictures for visual schedules.

- Create pictures and schedules on an iPad
- Search Google Images for the pictures you want to use and print them out
- Purchase ready-made laminated pictures
- Use online software to create and print out pictures
- Take photos of your own child involved in the activities you want pictures for; develop or print out the pictures

Concerning creating a visual schedule itself: If you use an iPad or tablet app, you can simply display the schedule right from the screen. If you make a schedule to hang up, it helps to laminate the schedule to avoid ripping or crumpling; or, you can Velcro or tape your pictures onto construction paper.

You can copy and paste pictures such as ones from Google Images or the ones in Clip Art (found in Microsoft Word) into a Microsoft Word table (of course, you can do this with your own pictures as well). If you want to show only a few pictures at a time, using Velcro might be the better option; but if you use a Microsoft Word table, you can cover some of the images with paper or create a few different mini-schedules with a few pictures in each. As stated previously, this may be beneficial for a child who gets overwhelmed with too many pictures at a time.

You can also purchase a ready-made schedule strip, schedule pocket chart, or magnetic schedule (all available online). For children who need to alternate between preferred and non-preferred activities or who need to know what is happening first and then next, and may be confused by a visual schedule with more than two pictures, you can create a "first/then" board, displaying only two items from the schedule with the words "First" and "Then" over them.

Keep in mind that children often benefit from removing or crossing off what they have already completed in their schedule. If you have removable pictures or words (Velcroed, taped, etc.), allow the child to take the piece off the schedule board and put it in an envelope, bin, etc., that is fastened near the schedule. Some pocket charts have a pocket at the bottom in which to put completed items.

If you find daily schedules too overwhelming,

sometimes a quick mini-schedule can be helpful for the moment. What is great about mini-schedules is that you can quickly draw pictures and/or write or type them on a piece of paper, your phone, a white board, etc., and simply erase or check off as you go.

For some children, pictures and writing help. Other children can benefit from having things written down for them (or writing it down themselves). It can be seen as a mini-schedule or a checklist. For example, it may include the next four things coming up, such as,

- Get dressed
- Brush teeth
- Eat breakfast
- Free time (e.g., watch TV, use tablet, play a game, etc.)

A study of Harvard graduates, from their Masters in Business Administration program, showed that of students who set goals for themselves, the three percent who were most successful in accomplishing those goals (at a ten-year follow up) were the ones who wrote them down (or drew them). This is a great strategy for children and adults.

Remember to build those preferred activities into the mini-schedule.

14. WAYS TO USE TIMERS TO ENCOURAGE HOMEWORK AND CHORE COMPLETION

Some children have difficulty working for prolonged periods of time without a break. They may get frustrated or mentally drained. I have seen children start to look around, talk, and play with items during prolonged periods of homework or class work. This often leads to an adult telling them to get back to work before they are mentally ready. Sometimes the child becomes resistant and refuses to get back to work. Other times they make statements such as "I am too tired," "It is too hard," "I am bored," or "I don't care about this." If they do get back to work, they may work slowly, or rush through the assignment, or not put forth their best effort. Timers are an excellent way to motivate your child or student(s) to complete tasks and follow directions.

Research supports the benefit of using timers with children diagnosed with Autism Spectrum Disorder (ASD). For example, a 2012 study completed at Apple Tree Learning Center, in Washington DC, concluded that, with a preschool student with a developmental delay, using a timer with a picture schedule significantly increased their time on task during center-based play. (Be sure to check the end of this chapter for types of timers to use with children who may have trouble understanding the countdown on a traditional digital timer).

Below I discuss three ways for you to effectively use timers with children to increase cooperation, time on-task, task completion, etc. *Side Note:* There is no magic fix. What works for one child may not work for another. If you have significant concerns about your child's ability, motivation, learning, behavior, or level of attention, talk to your child's doctor and/or school to find out what support they can provide.

So how can timers help?

1. Tell your child that they need to complete a certain amount of work and allow them to work towards a break. For example, if your child is given 20 math problems for homework, you can say, "Complete the first ten problems and then take a five-minute break to do something of your choice. Then do the next ten problems." During the break, set the timer for five minutes and make sure the child can see it so they know exactly how much time they have left.

This is a great method for encouraging work completion because children like to work towards something fun. Many children also need a mental break and will work more effectively when they have the opportunity to take one. Using a timer takes the ownership away from the parent or teacher. The adult is not arbitrarily telling the child that the break is over. The timer dictates the length of the break. This leads to less resistance from the child.

If you are doing an open ended activity, such as studying or practicing an academic skill, try setting the timer for ten minutes and saying something like "We will practice for ten minutes, take a five-minute break to do something of your choice, and practice for another ten minutes." In this case you would use the timer to let the child know how long the practice/study session will last and how long the break will last. Some children need suggestions for the break (e.g., "When you take your break do you want to draw or play a game on the computer?"). If you are offering suggestions, pick things that you know your child would want to work toward. Also, because some children can work for longer periods than others, and some benefit from longer breaks than others, you can adjust the number of minutes as necessary. Work with your child/student to see how much time works best for them.

A simple list of the plan can be extremely helpful:

- Ten math problems

- Five-minute break for a preferred activity
- Ten math problems
- Finished (pick activity of choice)

Children who struggle with reading/language may need the list to be in visual form. See Chapter 14: "How to Use Schedules to Improve Children's Behavior" for more on this topic.

2. Some children benefit from timer games. Children can become easily distracted during such routine tasks as getting dressed, putting toys away, or copying down their spelling words. The child may look around, talk, or play with items rather than getting the task done. If the child is able to do the task competently but easily gets distracted, they may benefit from a "timer game." For instance, you can tell your child that if they finish putting away their toys by the time the timer goes off, they can engage in an activity of their choice when they is done. You may want to time the fun activity they choose if you want them to do something else afterwards (e.g., put their toys away before the timer goes off, play on the computer for 20 minutes, get ready for bed). If "timer games" make your child anxious, keep in mind that if you do not want to turn it into a game you can say something like "You have ten minutes to put your toys away," and then set the timer to help your child monitor how much time they to complete the task.

3. Use timers to facilitate transitions from one activity to the next. Has your child ever resisted when

you told them to clean up, get off the computer, or turn off the television? Children often have difficulty breaking away from something enjoyable when they are not prepared for their fun time to come to an end. Using a timer is a great way to prepare your child for these situations. For example, you can set the timer and say, "In five minutes it is time to turn off the computer and start your homework."

Teachers can also use timers in their classrooms with individual students, or with the whole class, to encourage class work completion, using the same strategies described above.

For children who have trouble understanding the concept of time or numbers, a visual timer can be helpful because the child can see how much time is left. Visual timers can be purchased at online stores. Visual timers for kids include (1) a circular count-down display including a red disk that gradually disappears in a clockwise direction as time expires, (2) a set of multi-colored sand timers that let children know that time is up when the sand at the top gets to the bottom (with each color lasting for a fixed amount of time; for example, red is one minute, blue is five minutes, etc.), and (3) a timer app for an iPhone or iPad—such as one with a cute animal traveling from one place to another (the time is up upon arrival).

15. POSITIVE BEHAVIOR POETRY

One day while I sat in the waiting room of a doctor's office waiting for my appointment, I noticed a mother there with her little boy (around six years old). The mother was sitting in a chair looking at her phone while she and her son waited for the doctor to call them in. The little boy tried to interact with his mother in many positive ways ("Mommy, look at this" . . . "Mommy what do you think of this?" . . . "Mommy, can you read this to me?"), but she simply ignored him and looked at her phone.

It wasn't until he crawled under the office chairs, stood on the chairs, sang loudly, and ran in the waiting room that she shifted her attention to him. "Stop running!" "Be quiet!" "Get down from there!" "Get out of there!" It was witnessing this interaction, coupled with my training as a behavior specialist and school psychologist, that inspired me to write this poem!

Mommy, Can You See Me?

Mommy, Mommy, can you see me?
   I am playing nicely with my toys.
Mommy, can you hear me?
   I'm trying not to make a lot of noise.
Mommy, did you notice?
   I shared my candy with my brother.
Mommy, are you proud?
   I said, "Please may I have another?"
I thought that's what you wanted
   but you didn't even smile.
Learning how to make you happy
   might just take awhile.
You noticed when I threw my toys.
   You yelled at me that day.
You noticed when I was playing loud.
   You took my toys away.
You put me in the corner
   because I didn't share.
When I didn't use my manners,
   you gave me an evil stare.
Please help me understand
   how I'm supposed to act.
When I do the wrong things,
   that's when you react.
I just want you to see me,

and I know how to make you look.
When I act like I'm supposed to,
    all you do is stare at Facebook.
Mommy, can't you see?
    I just want you to notice.
I might learn to be a good kid
    if you learn to shift your focus.

Rachel Wise is a certified school psychologist and licensed behavior specialist with a master's degree in education. She is also the head author and CEO at Education and Behavior (educationandbehavior.com), an online research-based library for parents, educators, therapists, and counselors to find valuable information to effectively support children. Rachel has been working with individuals with academic and behavioral needs for over 20 years and has a passion for making a positive difference in the lives of children and the adults who support them. Rachel is also a proud mom to two wonderful children, a six-year-old boy (JT) and two-year-old girl (Lainey). They are her inspiration, and they motivate Rachel to keep sharing information to make a positive difference for children around the world.

www.ingramcontent.com/pod-product-compliance
Lightning Source LLC
Chambersburg PA
CBHW051435150726

48000CB00005B/2107